WORKING FOR GOD

The Story of R. G. LeTourneau
and the University He Founded

LeTourneau University Press

LeTourneau University Press

Working for God
Copyright © 2019 by Center for Faith & Work at LeTourneau University
Requests for information should be addressed to:
Center for Faith & Work at LeTourneau University
2100 S. Mobberly, Longview, Texas 75602

Library of Congress Cataloging-in-Publication Data
Peel, Kathy
    Working for God: The Story of R. G. LeTourneau and the University He Founded

    ISBN: 978-0-9896479-3-9

Cover design: Jun Kim, Encore Multi-Media

Those who knew Robert Gilmore LeTourneau as a young boy were justifiably concerned about his future. The likelihood that a headstrong misfit and eighth-grade dropout could become a prolific inventor, renowned business leader and generous philanthropist would have seemed preposterous.

But not to God.

He delights to redeem our shortcomings and empower the most unlikely individuals to accomplish exceedingly more than they can imagine, rousing them to fulfill their God-given calling and bring Him glory.

That is what God did for R. G. LeTourneau.

This unique book presents the inspiring story of LeTourneau's God-empowered life, embraces his enduring legacy and celebrates the innovative university he founded.

Dr. William C. Peel
Executive Director
Center for Faith & Work
at LeTourneau University

WORKING FOR GOD

THE STORY OF
R. G. LETOURNEAU
AND THE
UNIVERSITY HE FOUNDED

1 A Storm Shaped the Future

The Blizzard of 1888 paralyzed the Northeast.

Gale-force winds and record snowfall collapsed telegraph lines, halted railways and stranded thousands of travelers for days on end. Hundreds of people perished, and thousands of cattle froze to death.

In Richford, Vermont, not far from the Canadian border, Caleb and Lizzie LeTourneau huddled in their farmhouse to wait out the March storm with their three children, ages 5, 3 and 1. Their fourth child, Robert Gilmore LeTourneau, was born nine months later on November 30, 1888.

The epic blizzard prompted innovations that shaped America's future. The need for underground rail lines and reliable communication infrastructure propelled civic leaders into action.

The blizzard also shaped the future of Caleb LeTourneau and his growing family.

A decade before the historic storm, family circumstances had thrust Caleb into an unchosen career.

Caleb's parents, Jean and Marie LeTourneau, were French Huguenot missionaries who started a boarding school in Richford, Vermont in 1857.

When ill health forced them to retire from teaching, Jean and Marie bought some land just north of town. Their two sons, Joshua and Caleb, helped them build a farmhouse and a sawmill by a stream that traversed the property.

First-born Joshua was destined to run the family farm and sawmill, while his younger brother Caleb would train for the ministry. But plans changed when Joshua lost an arm in a sawmill accident, and the mantle passed to Caleb.

In 1880, Elizabeth (Lizzie) Lorimer caught Caleb's eye at church. They married on Christmas Day, 1881. The newlyweds moved into the LeTourneau farmhouse and started their family. During the life-threatening blizzard in 1888, Caleb began to dream of a better life in a warmer climate. Later that year, a few weeks after baby Robert's birth, Caleb stepped toward his dream.

He packed up Lizzie and their four children for an extended stay at her parents' home in Quebec. Then, he boarded a train and headed south with Robert Gilmore, his best friend and newborn son's namesake. Caleb and Robert traveled to Baja California, where they put down money to buy two farms.

On their journey back home, they stopped to visit Caleb's brother, Joshua, who had moved to Duluth, Minnesota after the sawmill accident. In 1889, Duluth was producing more millionaires per capita than any other U.S. city, thanks to abundant natural resources, a busy harbor and ship canal, and the Great Northern Railroad.

Joshua had built a lucrative career in the printing industry, and he had plans in hand to build a large house overlooking Lake Superior. Imagine his delight when his brother Caleb and Robert Gilmore—two of Vermont's best craftsmen—showed up at his door. Joshua offered them cash on the spot to stay in Duluth long enough to build his home.

The elegant craftsmanship of Joshua's home launched Caleb into a career as a building contractor in Duluth. In 1890, Lizzie and the children joined him there.

Caleb never returned to balmy Baja, but God used the Blizzard of 1888 and his dream for a better life to steer his family to Minnesota. There, God began to shape young R. G. LeTourneau into the man who would become the best-known Christian businessman of his day.

No dream is too big or too small for God.

Imagination is a powerful gift from God. It propels us to dream about the future and envision the world as God meant it to be. We long for a better life because we were created to live in a perfect world, and someday we will.

Psalm 37:4 says God will plant His desires in our heart if we delight in Him. Sometimes, God plants colossal-size dreams—about a new technology or a cure for chronic disease, for example. He also plants dreams that, in comparison, may seem small—such as the desire for fulfilling work or a good education. But these are big dreams as well, because they can have far-reaching, multi-generational impact.

Any size dream may be a clue to God's purposes for an individual or a family.

Above: Rubber stamp (reversed) from J. J. LeTourneau Printing Company in Duluth

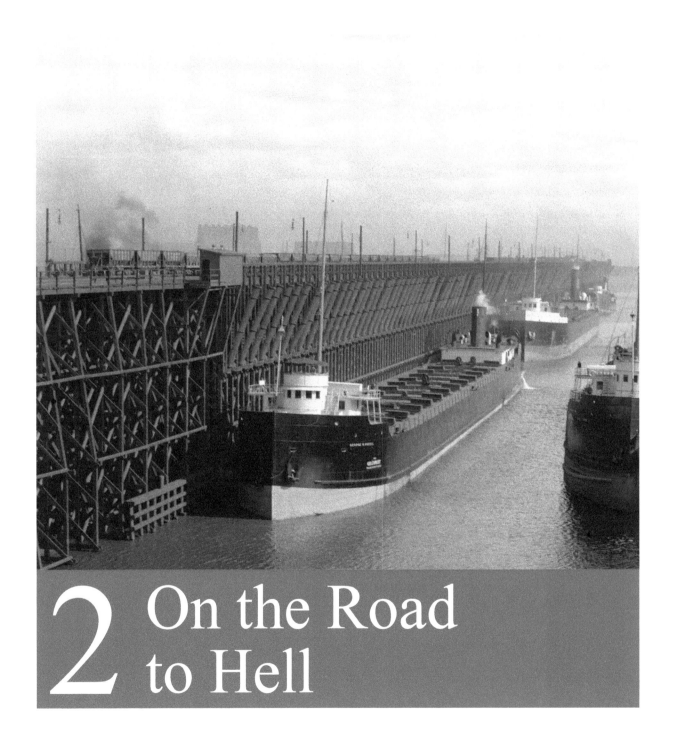

2 On the Road to Hell

At the turn of the century, Duluth rivaled New York as America's busiest port.

Lake Superior's North Shore and Duluth's bustling harbor provided widespread adventure and opportunities for R. G. LeTourneau to learn about the world during his formative years—age 2 to 14.

Near his home, cascading streams forged nearby forests and spilled into the world's largest freshwater lake. Steam-belching locomotives and enormous ships moved masses of lumber, grain, coal and ore through a complex of piers, railways, elevators and berths. Looking back at these years of his life, he wrote,

The man who brought the ore trains out on the long trestle and dumped them into the hoppers that fed the ore to the boats below must be, I thought, the happiest man in the world.

Opposite page: Duluth Ore Docks, early 1900s

Caleb LeTourneau's household continued to grow and fill the home he built for his family near the lake. By 1900, 12-year-old Bob (his family moniker) was one of eight children. As his body grew to man-size height and girth, his inborn stubborn streak also grew and became a lightning rod for family conflict.

Taunting Bob was a favorite pastime of his brothers. On one occasion, they built a barricade to keep him out of a certain room. In response, Bob used his brawn to shatter the door, which earned him the lion's share of the blame and punishment.

To my mother, I was restless, inquisitive, energetic, determined and ambitious. To my brothers, I was destructive, willful, stubborn and fanatically determined to amount to nothing.

Getting picked on by his siblings and unfairly punished by his parents was the norm—at least from Bob's perspective.

One day, when it was his turn to draw water from the well, he decided to enact revenge. He pumped out all the water, brought back an empty pail and reported (with some degree of truth) that the family's water source was dry.

Such antics invited regular chastisement from Caleb LeTourneau, whose rebukes often included Bible verses.

In the summer of 1901, things came to a head when Bob jumped head-first from a boulder into Lake Superior to show off for friends. Three feet below the surface, a jagged rock split Bob's head wide open, and the injury almost killed him. Sixteen stitches later, harsh words from his father amplified the pain.

Confined to bed rest, Bob wallowed in self-pity. He decided the only reasonable course of action for an unwanted, unloved boy was to run away from home.

One frosty autumn night a few weeks later, Bob made good on his decision. He walked out with only the clothes on his back. The moonless night and biting

The LeTourneau home was located in an undeveloped area of Duluth, which is now called Lakeside Lester Park. "I ran wild through the woods and along the lake shore," Bob wrote.

north wind hindered the runaway's progress. In his mind's eye, Bob saw packs of hungry wolves closing in, but he pressed on. About a mile from home, he located a familiar ravine and felt his way to a ledge which provided overnight shelter from the wind.

Cold and hungry the next morning, he walked to a widow's neighboring farm and asked if he could barter work for breakfast. She accepted his offer, and while he fed chickens and dug potatoes from her garden, the woman let Bob's parents know his whereabouts. The three agreed on a plan to let him stay at her farm in exchange for helping her with daily tasks.

Weeks passed before Bob recognized the pettiness of his attitude and actions. When he returned home and apologized, Caleb LeTourneau acknowledged his own role in the conflict and welcomed his prodigal son with open arms.

Bob is on the far right in this 1901 family photo. The diving accident scar is visible on his head.

Reconciliation between Bob and his father was a life-defining moment.

> *Discovering my father's love changed my whole attitude. The chores that I had hated and fought against resentfully, I now cheerfully did because I wanted to serve him.*

Although Bob's positive demeanor and cooperative spirit improved the atmosphere at the LeTourneau home, at school a storm was brewing.

Bob had made remarkable progress in his fifth-grade studies, so his teacher promoted him to the seventh grade—a decision that proved to be unwise. Bob was taller and heftier than his older classmates, yet he struggled with core subjects they had mastered in sixth grade.

I was not only the biggest in the class, but also the dumbest. I quit trying entirely, and came to hate school with an almost physical violence.

Lester Park School, 1898, where Bob and his siblings attended

One night, about halfway through his abysmal school year, hope appeared on Bob's horizon.

Caleb LeTourneau gathered his family for a big announcement: In late spring, they were leaving Duluth's brutal winters behind and moving 1,700 miles west to Portland, Oregon—where the economy was thriving and construction work abounded year round.

As far as Bob was concerned, this was fantastic news! He could leave his troubled past behind and look forward to a fresh start where no one knew him as "that stubborn LeTourneau kid."

I attended church regularly and heard a lot about God without learning a thing ... About all I knew of religion was that if you didn't have it you were going to Hell.

But young Bob did not yet understand that only God could give him the fresh start in life he needed.

Though he had clocked countless hours at church to please his family, Bob did not know God—nor did he care to.

Reminiscing over this season of life, he wrote, "I was definitely on the road to hell and working hard to stay there."

Unbeknownst to Bob, God was at work behind the scenes of his life, orchestrating circumstances and softening his heart to become a faithful follower of Christ.

God loves to transform our weaknesses into strengths that bring Him glory.

Bob's dare-devil propensity and single-minded stubbornness were character weaknesses that caused him and his family much angst and frustration.

In the coming years, God would transform Bob's nervy nature and pigheadedness into Spirit-powered perseverance to overcome and prevail over countless challenges in his business ventures and personal life.

"... he who began a good work in you will carry it on to completion until the day of Christ Jesus." (Philippians 1:6)

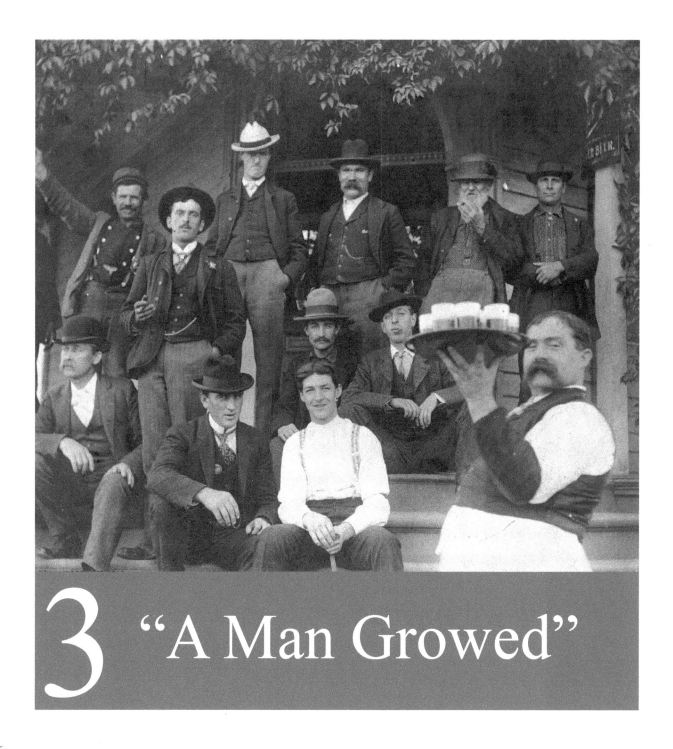

3 "A Man Growed"

In the early 1900s, Portland was known as the Unheavenly City.

Rapid population growth fueled boundless prosperity, as well as rampant crime and corruption. Business was booming at saloons, gambling parlors, opium dens and bordellos. Many establishments had trap-door access to an underground maze of tunnels created for easy escape during police raids.

The sights and sounds of Portland fascinated 14-year-old Bob LeTourneau and kept his parents on their knees.

School, however, held no fascination for Bob. He could not envision his 6-foot, 160-pound body crammed into a desk designed for eighth-graders.

Before school started, he mustered enough courage to announce to his father that he'd had enough schooling. "I'm a man growed," he argued relentlessly.

Opposite page: Men gathered at Groh's Saloon in Portland, 1903

Caleb LeTourneau wanted each of his children to earn a high-school diploma. But he was fighting an uphill battle with head-strong Bob and American culture.

In the early 1900s, 96 percent of working-class children, age 12 and older, dropped out of school. Eighteen percent of American workers at the time were under age 16.

Bob won the battle over school, but his father hatched a plan to win the war. One Sunday after church, Caleb explained his predicament to the owner of East Portland Iron Works, who agreed to hire Bob. The plan turned on the idea that a taste of adult responsibility— performing strenuous labor in stifling heat—would make school look appealing by comparison.

Both men, however, underestimated Bob's resolve.

Energized by what he was learning about molding and metallurgy, Bob labored diligently at his difficult job.

Typical foundry work in the early 1900s

"The Sunday Oregonian," March 12, 1905, Part 3, p.25

While Bob worked hard at the Portland foundry, the Spirit of God was at work almost 8,000 miles away in Wales, where more than 150,000 people professed faith in Christ during the 1904 Welch Revival. Effects of the revival rippled across the Atlantic and spawned a spiritual awakening in America.

In December 1904, Portland churches banded together for a week-long crusade, and droves of people trusted in Christ. By spring 1905, 240 stores and businesses jointly decided to close daily between 11 a.m. and 2 p.m. for prayer.

One of the individuals who came to Christ during the Portland crusade was 16-year-old Bob LeTourneau.

> *No bolts of lightning hit me. ... I just prayed to the Lord to save me, and then I was aware of another Presence. No words were spoken. I received no messages ... all my bitterness was drained away, and I was filled with such a vast relief that I could not contain it all.*

Bob's parents rejoiced to learn that God had answered their prayers.

19

In fall 1905, Bob's career at East Portland Iron Works ended abruptly when fire destroyed the foundry. After a long, fruitless job search in Portland, he learned of an opening at a San Francisco foundry.

The 18-year-old "man growed" packed his belongings, moved to California and wasted no time settling in. He found a room to rent, got involved at a church and enrolled at a vocational school—which, to his surprise, he enjoyed immensely because his foundry work gave hands-on context to his studies.

On April 18, 1906, a few months into his new life, Bob awoke before dawn to what sounded like bombs exploding all around him. The Great San Francisco Earthquake struck the coast of Northern California with an estimated magnitude of 7.8.

Fires burned for days, leaving 80 percent of San Francisco in ruins. An estimated 3,000 people died in the disaster, but God spared Bob's life. Later, he recalled,

> *From the hills in back of my friend's home we and thousands of refugees watched the city burn. For several days we got our food by standing in a breadline and taking what they handed to us.*

Five days after the earthquake, Bob wrote to his family and let them know that he was alive and unhurt.

I awoke with a start about fifteen minutes after five. The house was being jerked back and forth ... The house sank three or four feet. Almost entirely demolished the first floor and then toppled over against the next house ...

Read the full text of Bob's letter to his family at https://centerforfaithandwork.com/SFEathquake.

After the earthquake, money was tight and jobs were scarce. Bob found temporary work at two foundries and an elevator manufacturer. When those jobs played out and prospects looked dim, he accepted an offer from his brother Bill, who needed stumps pulled on acreage he owned in Rex, Oregon.

The back-breaking work prompted Bob to create an easier way to get the job done. He bought a used steam engine and a few drums of cable to concoct a machine to pull the stumps. But when he tested his invention, it backfired and knocked out his front teeth.

This incident sent him back to San Francisco for porcelain crowns that consumed all the money he had earned pulling stumps. Once again, Bob was back on the street, searching for work in the Bay City. This time, he was hired by Yerba Buena Power System to scrape and refurbish old batteries. The dirty, dangerous job lasted only three months, but during his time at Yerba Buena, Bob offered to help with other projects, which allowed him to learn the fundamentals of electrical engineering and become proficient with an oxyhydrogen welding torch.

About this time, Caleb and Joshua LeTourneau moved their families to the San Joaquin Valley to try their hand at farming and gold mining. Bob worked for his father and uncle, helping them out with various tasks. One day he gashed his leg to the bone with an ax, which sidelined him yet again.

While his leg healed, 21-year-old Bob said he felt like a washed-up bum. He longed for a stable career, unaware that God was using every experience to prepare him for his holy calling as an inventor and entrepreneur.

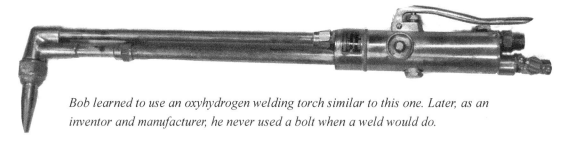

Bob learned to use an oxyhydrogen welding torch similar to this one. Later, as an inventor and manufacturer, he never used a bolt when a weld would do.

Every individual is uniquely designed by God in His image.

Countless books, workshops and assessment tools can help us discover a career path. But most of these methods miss something important: We come into the world with God-given abilities that He bestowed on us to fulfill His purposes. In Psalm 139, David reflected on this truth.

For you created my inmost being; you knit me together in my mother's womb. I praise you because I am fearfully and wonderfully made...

Each of us has an important role to play in God's plan. To discover our vocational calling, we must understand our unique design. When we identify and use our God-given gifts, we experience joy, do our best work and bring glory to God.

For we are his workmanship, created in Christ Jesus for good works, which God prepared beforehand, that we should walk in them. (Ephesians 2:10)

4 Called to Business

Bob brought an unquenchable desire to learn to every job he tackled.

Though his formal education ended after the seventh grade, Bob had gained skills working as an apprentice ironmonger, lead burner, bricklayer, carpenter, gold miner, stump puller, ditch digger, wood chopper, farmer and battery refurbisher—all by age 21.

He had also enrolled in correspondence courses to learn geometry, trigonometry, mechanical engineering, as well as auto mechanics—for which he awarded himself a "Bachelor of Motorcycles" degree.

Bob hoped to get a job as an auto mechanic, but garage owners were unimpressed with his self-conferred degree. Unable to find work as a mechanic, he hired on with a construction company charged with building a bridge over the Stanislaus River near Stockton, California.

When the bridge was completed, Bob found work at a garage in Stockton, where his skills earned him great favor with customers. In 1911, at age 23, he had the opportunity to co-own a garage in equal partnership with an acquaintance. The pair opened Superior Garage and enjoyed immediate success. Soon, they expanded their business to include a Regal auto dealership.

At county fairs across the country, automakers showcased new models and staged races to attract crowds. For the 1912 San Joaquin County Fair, Superior Garage hired a professional to drive a car Bob had souped up for the race. During a test drive around the track, Bob was in the passenger seat when the driver lost control and wrecked the car. The crash left Bob with a broken neck.

Back then, few people survived a broken neck, and doctors knew little about traction. Recovery and rehabilitation took many months, and Bob's head leaned to the right for the rest of his life. But something wonderful happened during his convalescence: He met the love of his life, Evelyn Peterson.

The New SAXON – $395

Best Two-Passenger Automobile in the World at Anywhere Near Its Price

In 1914, Superior Garage dropped its Regal dealership in favor of the up-and-coming Saxon.

Bob at Superior Garage in Stockton, California, 1911

In August 1917, five months after the U.S. entered World War I, Bob and Evelyn married. The newlyweds agreed that Bob should serve in the country's war effort, but lingering effects from his broken neck disqualified him from military service.

Undeterred, Bob arranged with his business partner to run the garage while he offered his services as a mechanic and welder at Mare Island Navy Yard, north of San Francisco.

On weekends, Bob commuted back to the farmhouse Evelyn had secured for them near Stockton. In spring 1918, they learned she was expecting their first child.

In September 1918, the Spanish Influenza Pandemic hit Mare Island, and Bob fell victim. The deadly flu infected an estimated 500 million people worldwide, killing between 20 to 50 million.

Bob was burning up with fever when he collapsed on a cot at the Mare Island hospital and heard a doctor say, "Come quick, this fellow's about gone."

A hospital worker gave Bob an injection, and his fever broke. The following week he was back on the job.

It is likely that Bob was one of 40 deathly ill men who received injections formulated by Dr. Richard Neilson, the Navy surgeon credited with conquering the flu epidemic at Mare Island.

Mare Island Boys Conquer Influenza With Neilson Cure

Special Dispatch to the Chronicle

VALLEJO, October 26.—Surgeon John L. Neilson, U.S.N. in charge of the medical supply depot at Mare Island, is the man who is said to have conquered the influenza and pneumonia at the navy yard. His cure consists of injections of sodium salicylate as well as magnesium sulphate solutions into the veins of the patients at different intervals. The cure has been such a success that the epidemic scare is over at the yard and one of the hospitals has already been torn down.

According to Dr. Neilson, the injections were used in forty bad cases, all of whom are able to be out and around at the present time.

Bob was still at Mare Island on October 30, 1918, when Evelyn gave birth to their first son. Less than two weeks later, the Allies and Germany signed an armistice agreement, marking the end of World War I. Bob returned home the following week—overjoyed to see Evelyn and meet their 3-week-old son, whom they named Caleb after Bob's father.

Bob's first week back at home was a time of celebration over their new son and the war's end.

But his first day back at Superior Garage, Bob's joy turned to despair. He learned that during his time working at Mare Island, his business partner had spent scads of money, wining and dining potential customers (and himself), and had driven the garage and auto business to the brink of bankruptcy.

His partner had not bothered to keep track of expenses or any revenue that had come in, so the financial records were in chaos. It took Bob weeks to find all the bills and assess the damage. He wrote,

Every day brought more discouragement, and by the end of January, after the longest hours and hardest work I had ever done in my life, I thought I was about as low as a man can get.

Although Bob thought things couldn't get any worse, he returned home late one night and found Evelyn pacing the floor, waiting for the doctor to arrive. The flu epidemic was ravaging Stockton, and 3-month-old Caleb became infected. He died February 11, 1919.

Brokenhearted and numb with grief, Bob cried out to God for the courage to keep going.

Bob was able to dissolve the garage partnership by assuming $5,000 of the company's debt to creditors. To begin paying down the debt, he took a job repairing a man's rundown Holt tractor. In a week's time, Bob had the tractor humming.

But something else important happened that week: Bob recognized that a clunky old machine had captured his imagination, and the task of getting it to run smoothly gave him a sense of joy and satisfaction.

Though the tractor seemed good as new, the owner was suspicious. He proposed a deal for Bob to use the repaired tractor and a scraper to level a 40-acre section of his property. If the tractor was still running after a week, he would pay the repair bill, plus $1 dollar for every hour Bob worked.

Bob accepted the offer and fulfilled his part of the agreement. The owner paid up and then asked Bob to overhaul all kinds of equipment—which was like letting a kid loose in a candy store. As he worked on the machines, Bob's mind whirred about how to improve them.

But at the end of each day, reality set in. He was receiving minimal pay for his work, and he had barely dented his looming debt. Plus, Evelyn was pregnant with their second child. Worries about money and concern for how he would support his family consumed the mind of 31-year-old Bob.

When his sister Sarah, a missionary to China, visited Stockton she pointed out to Bob that his mind was on everything except serving Christ. Sarah's words stung but rang true and prompted him to attend church revival meetings every night for a week.

One night, Bob knelt at the altar and committed his life wholly to Christ. He experienced a fresh sense of God's presence, but he also felt uneasy and uncertain about what it meant "to go all out for God."

The commonly held assumption that serving God with one's whole heart meant becoming a preacher, an evangelist or a missionary produced no small amount of angst in a man who loved machines and dreamed of developing better ways to move dirt.

Bob felt confused and conflicted over what God wanted him to do, so he asked his pastor for advice.

I know a layman can't serve God like a preacher can. But tell me, does He want me to be a missionary?

After they prayed together, the pastor told Bob that God needs businessmen, as well as preachers and missionaries. Surprised by his words, Bob responded,

All right, if that is what God wants me to be, I'll try to be His businessman.

God values all types of work.

Many Christians think only those who work at a church, a mission agency or a Christian organization are "working for God." But this is contrary to scripture.

Whatever you do, work at it with all your heart, as working for the Lord. (Colossians 3:23)

Reformation leader Martin Luther asked his parishioners to consider all of the workers God used to provide the breakfast they thanked Him for each morning.

Today, God uses farmers, ranchers, truckers, dairy workers, supermarket owners, butchers, bakers and cashiers, as well as engineers who design farm equipment, construction workers who build highways and bankers who provide capital—to name a few.

Everyone who meets legitimate human needs is working for God.

5 Changing the Face of the Earth

Bob's new perspective of business shaped his future.

In early 1920, 32-year-old Bob took a step of faith: He asked God to be his Business Partner and launched a land-leveling business, based on three compelling factors.

First, he understood that he could serve God through business. Second, he loved moving dirt, and he was fascinated with machines—repairing them, watching them work and pondering how they could work better. Third, the potential for building a successful business as a contractor was excellent, given where he lived.

God had prepared Bob for this moment through an unorthodox education and many character-building experiences. Also, it was no accident that he settled in Stockton, nestled in the San Joaquin Valley, which was fast becoming the "food basket of the world."

And, thanks to inventor-entrepreneurs like Daniel Best and Benjamin Holt, agriculture mechanization pioneers, the region was also the earthmoving capital of America at the time.

Opposite page: Bob waving from the top of a LeTourneau machine behind the Longview plant, 1961

To start the business, Bob needed equipment. He mustered enough money for a down payment on a used 1915 Holt tractor and bartered repair work in exchange for use of a friend's scraper. Then, he mortgaged almost everything he and Evelyn owned against a $1,000 bank loan for working capital.

On his first job at a nearby ranch, it took two men to operate his equipment—one to drive the tractor and one to operate the scraper blade controls. Atop his tractor, Bob couldn't help but think there had to be a more efficient way to level a field. One day an idea emerged in his mind.

He bought a generator and two electric motors at a war surplus sale and worked every night for two weeks to bring his idea to life. He welded the motors and rack-and-pinion gears on the scraper

to move the blade up and down. He mounted the generator on the tractor frame to power the motors.

To his astonishment, the contraption worked better than he thought it would. And best of all, it only required one person to operate it. He described his invention as,

>...a sort of mongrel drag scraper; part Fresno, part conventional scraper, part scoop.

His newfangled machine allowed him to move more dirt faster than anyone in history, so business started rolling in.

Bob on his Holt 75 tractor pulling his first scraper, known as a full-drag scraper, 1921

In 1921, Bob bought a small house with a barn on an acre of land in Stockton. He converted the barn into a machine shop and used the land for an open-air factory and assembly yard where he implemented ideas to improve his first scrapers. As he built new and improved machines, he sold the old ones to farmers in the area.

In 1926, Bob received his first major contract to build a highway between Stockton and Oakland, and more big jobs followed.

In Bob's mind, he was primarily an earthmoving contractor who kept improving his machines for his own benefit. But his perception changed in 1929 when he received an order for a machine from a contractor in Russia. That year he incorporated as R. G. LeTourneau, Inc.

Bob's business continued to grow, but so did his debt. By mid-1932, he couldn't make payroll, and creditors crouched at his door. Plus, he and Evelyn now had five children. In the midst of the Great Depression, Bob had plenty of reasons to be depressed. But he also had a Business Partner he could turn to for help.

In late 1932, things turned around. Bob captured industry attention by putting his earthmoving machines on pneumatic tires, enabling them to go

Shop and assembly plant behind Bob and Evelyn's home in Stockton, around 1928

almost anywhere. In 1933, he closed the contracting end of his company to focus his attention on manufacturing. By 1934, sales neared $1 million, with net profit around $340,000. To sustain growth, he needed another factory.

Caterpillar, a key sales ally, suggested that Bob build a plant near their headquarters in Peoria, Illinois. This made sense, so in January 1935, he bought 23 acres along the Illinois River.

In April, Bob and some of his management team boarded a freight train loaded with machine tools. They arrived in Peoria after a two-week deluge had turned the plant site into a muddy quagmire. Bob realized he had not asked about the river's flood stage when he bought the property. Plus, there was no side rail or crane for unloading the machines nor a building to store them.

Never one to waste time blaming or complaining, Bob got busy. While his team unloaded the machines needed to build a side rail, he sketched a design for a crane that could be welded around the chassis of a tractor. In three days, his crew had unloaded all the equipment and moved it to high ground.

Within a month, they had constructed a 100- by 300-foot factory with an open-air production line and manufactured 13 large scrapers.

Employees in Peoria began calling Bob "Mr. R. G." after Rube Goldberg, the Pulitzer Prize-winning journalist and illustrator known for his zany invention cartoons.

Evelyn and their six children, age 1 to 15, arrived soon after Bob. They moved into a home big enough for their family of eight, plus room to accommodate guests who visited frequently.

Locating in Peoria was good for business. As Bob designed and built new machines, sales grew exponentially. In 1938, they broke ground for a third plant in Toccoa, Georgia, and over the next decade, he established manufacturing plants in Rydalmere, Australia; Vicksburg, Mississippi; Stockton-on-Tees, England; and Longview, Texas.

When World War II broke out, earth-moving equipment had become as important as guns, ships and planes. R. G. LeTourneau, Inc. supplied 70 percent of the earth-moving equipment used by the U.S. military and its allies on all fronts. LeTourneau machines uprooted jungles, built roads and airstrips in the Pacific islands, and cleared battle rubble in France, Sicily, Italy and Africa.

Major General Eugene Reybold of the Army Corps of Engineers remarked, "Victory seems to favor the side with the greater ability to move dirt."

Top right: Seabees in the 62nd Naval Construction Battalion build an airstrip on Iwo Jima using LeTourneau LP Carryall scrapers. Seabees built 235,000 roads, 400 bases, 100 air strips, 700 acres of warehouses and housing for 1.5 million personnel, as the Navy and Marines island-hopped toward Tokyo.

Bottom right: Soldiers watch an Army Corps of Engineers bulldozer, fitted with a LeTourneau CK7 blade, fill bomb craters in Normandy.

During World War II, R. G. LeTourneau Inc. produced 10,000 Carryalls, 14,000 bulldozers, 1,600 sheepfoot rollers, 1,200 rooters and 1,800 Tournapulls for America's military. When the war ended, these machines became war-surplus items, flooding the market with LeTourneau equipment.

New production was scaled back, which turned the company's balance sheet red. Once again, Bob put his God-given ingenuity to work.

A post-war demand for paper required moving mountains of wood for pulp, so Bob designed and built machines to meet the needs of America's lumber industry.

This effort put the company back in the black by 1947, around the time another national need surfaced. America's infrastructure—our roads, bridges, airports, water and electrical systems—suffered from deferred maintenance. Everything needed to be updated and expanded. This titanic national endeavor would require, literally, changing the face of the earth.

To meet this need, 59-year-old Bob designed a bigger scraper, which allowed LeTourneau machines to play a key role in creating America's Interstate Highway System.

In 1953, a number of acquisition suitors approached Bob. After prayer, he sold the earth-moving division of his company to Westinghouse Air Brake Company for $31 million.

The deal specified that Bob not manufacture earth-moving equipment for five years at the Vicksburg and Longview plants, which were not included in the acquisition. And, at Bob's request, Westinghouse agreed that all employees at the acquired plants could keep their jobs.

During the five non-compete years, Bob invented an electric-wheel power system and monster machines that could crush giant trees, haul loads of logs, pull land trains over snow and sand, and cast a concrete house in one pour. But the market for this type of equipment was smaller than expected, which throttled cash flow once again.

Right: In 1948, the Israeli Army captured Beer Sheva, a dusty desert village with 200 inhabitants. The army bought LeTourneau equipment to build concrete houses and infrastructure, allowing Beer Sheva to grow into a business and cultural center, and home to 1 million people today. In the photo, Golda Meir, Israel's future Prime Minister, inspects progress in Beer Sheva.

Below: Bob demonstrates his electric wheel at a Chicago convention.

By their mid-60s, many people begin to slow down. But not Bob. He geared up and designed an electric-powered mobile off-shore oil-drilling platform on retractable 140-foot legs. He sold the invention to the president of Zapata Oil Company, George H. W. Bush. The rig, christened the "The Scorpion" in 1956, revolutionized offshore petroleum exploration and drilling.

By 1970, the LeTourneau name was on more than half of the offshore drilling platforms around the world.

To millions of people, Bob was known as "The Dean of Earthmoving" and a mechanical genius whose machines contributed greatly to America's national defense and highway infrastructure.

Over his lifetime, he was granted 299 patents relating to earthmoving equipment, manufacturing processes and machine tools. Despite numerous awards, accolades and acclaim, he always described himself as "a mechanic whom the Lord has blessed."

George H.W. Bush and George W. Bush at the Scorpion's christening, Galveston, Texas, 1956

Typical LeTourneau Jack-Up Rig

God works through business to fulfill His purposes for creation.

The products we create and the services we perform are the means God ordained to develop His creation and foster human flourishing. Bob put it this way:

When God created the world and everything in it, He didn't mean for us stop there and say, "God, you've done it all. There's nothing left for us to build." He wanted us to take off from there and really build for His greater glory.

From this perspective, all work that meets legitimate human needs takes on a larger purpose. A baker contributes beautiful desserts that enhance important life celebrations. A banker facilitates the home-buying process so families have a place to blossom. A sanitation worker plays a vital role in the community's health and welfare.

All good work, well done, brings glory to God and blesses His world.

Two things I like most to do: one is to design machines, turn on the power, and see them work. The other is to help turn on the power of the gospel and see it work in the lives of people.
—R. G. LeTourneau

6 Business by the Book

Every Christian's work is a holy calling.

In 1919, when 31-year-old Bob committed his life wholly to God, he had lots to learn. He recognized that his call to business was a holy calling, but he had to figure out how to integrate his faith with his work—and he didn't have a how-to manual or a mentor to model what this looked like every day on the job.

What Bob did have was faith that God cared about his work on Monday just as much as He cared about his worship on Sunday. He also had his Bible, and he was confident that his new Business Partner would guide him day by day. He explained,

> *I was just a mechanic striving to translate His laws in terms of machinery, and as long as I understood I was just His follower, and didn't get to thinking I was operating under my own head of steam, I was on the right track.*

From Day One of his commitment to be God's businessman, faith informed how Bob worked and lived. Most days, he stuck close to God, drew on God's wisdom and gave God the glory for his success and achievements.

However, Bob was quick to admit there were many days when he strayed from God, relied on human wisdom and neglected to give God glory for his accomplishments. But faith guided those days as well. Bob trusted in God's unconditional love and knew he could return to God, confess his prideful attitudes and receive forgiveness.

Bob never doubted God's goodness, though his spiritual journey was filled with pain and difficulty. For example,

- He almost died in the Spanish Influenza Pandemic of 1918.
- His first-born son died at 3 months from the flu, and his second-born son died at age 19 in a plane crash.
- At age 49, he came close to death in a car crash that killed five people.
- He teetered near bankruptcy numerous times.

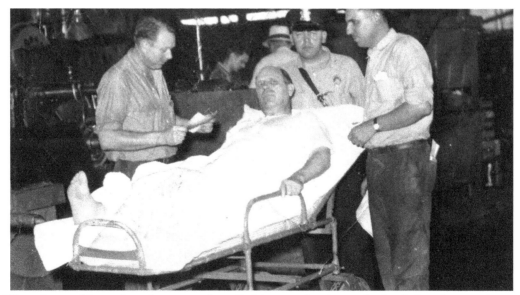

When shattered bones from the car crash put Bob in casts for six months, he designed a stretcher that could be wheeled around the Peoria plant. He endured residual pain for the rest of his life.

Today, many Christians puzzle over how to live out their faith at work. Although every workplace is distinctive, wisdom gleaned from how Bob integrated faith into his daily work provides inspiration and guidance for Christians in every type of work.

Bob believed that God cared about every aspect of his work. He explained,

> When you go into partnership with God, you've got a Partner closer and more active than any human partner you can ever get.

> He participates fully in everything you let Him do, and when you start putting on airs and thinking you're doing it with your own head of steam, He can set you down quicker and harder than a thunderbolt.

> There's nothing dull about being in partnership with God

Through bottomed-out economies, personal catastrophe, bad business partners, short deadlines, breakdowns and hard decisions, LeTourneau knew who God was, so he knew who he was.

—Dr. Dale A. Lunsford
President, LeTourneau University

Bob faced financial ruin many times in his career. On one occasion, he got down on his knees and prayed,

> Don't let me down now, Lord. I've got all this work, and if You let me down, I'm ruined.

As he prayed, Bob saw his mistake.

> Strike that out, Lord. I didn't mean that. I'm not asking You not to let me down. I'm asking You to help me not let You down. I'm not asking to use You. I'm asking You to use me.

His attitude changed.

> All wrapped up in my petty problems, I had once more begun to think I was working for myself instead of the Lord.

> I slept well that night, and when I woke up, I had the answer to my problem.

He helped employees flourish vocationally. Bob regularly walked around the plants to encourage employees and help them understand their value to the company and the vital role they played in each project.

When he learned that some of his employees did not understand basic fractions and decimals, Bob hired tutors and provided correspondence courses in math and other subjects. Around 1,500 employees in Peoria and Toccoa took advantage of these courses.

He helped employees flourish spiritually. Bob pioneered the practice of employing company chaplains at all LeTourneau factories. The chaplains held Bible studies and helped employees with emotional and spiritual needs. Optional religious services were held between shifts in plant cafeterias, which were furnished with a platform, a podium and an altar.

He went above and beyond to meet employees' physical needs. Four hundred employees built the plant at Toccoa, Georgia. Some workers came from Peoria, others from the Toccoa region—and they all needed housing, food and other necessities. To meet these needs, Bob organized a company to create a community for employees.

He acquired 4,500 acres, bought a herd of registered cattle, built a dairy, purchased a canning factory and started a bus line between Toccoa and the new plant. He also erected prefabricated steel houses and, later, concrete houses that employees could rent for cost. He built similar communities in Vicksburg and Longview.

The first concrete home in the Vicksburg LeTourneau community, November 1945

Above: Employees gather for chapel at the Peoria plant, around 1943.

Right: Bob greets an apprentice at the plant in Rydalmere, Australia, 1949.

He helped Christians see business as a holy calling and encouraged them to be ambassadors for Christ in their work. Bob built relationships with other Christian leaders who were committed to helping people integrate their faith and work.

He led the steering committee that directed the early years of the Christian Business Men's Committee (CBMC, and he served as president of the Gideons.

If I had a religion that limped along during the week, and maybe worked only on Sunday, or while you're in church, I don't think I'd be very sold on it.

I think I'd turn it in on a new model that worked seven days a week, that would work when I was at church, in my home, or out at the plant. And that is what Christianity does.

Bob viewed Christians in the workplace as God's instruments to bring the gospel to the world. In a speech to Peoria's Chamber of Commerce, he said,

Preachers can tell us that Christianity works. They are God's salesmen ... but unless we businessmen testify that Christianity is the driving power of our business, you'll always have doubters claiming religion is all talk and no production.

He believed all of creation belongs to God, and we are His stewards. In 1935, Bob and Evelyn capped their lifestyle, established the LeTourneau Foundation, and placed 90 percent of the corporate stock in the foundation.

In 1944, a *Life* magazine article recognized the LeTourneau Foundation as America's largest religious foundation.

When asked why he gave away so much of the company's profits, Bob explained,

> *The question is not how much of my money do I give to God, but how much of His money do I keep for myself?*

He blessed the communities where he opened plants. Bob believed if a church could be dedicated to the Lord, so could a factory. Employees, city officials and dignitaries who attended dedication ceremonies heard Bob share the gospel message and explain what it meant to have God as his Business Partner.

In 1938, for the plant dedication in Toccoa, Bob and Evelyn provided 20 hogs, 30 sheep, 1,400 pounds of beef and thousands of bottles of soft drinks. For a week following the event, revival services were held on the plant grounds and hundreds of people trusted Christ.

> *When Mr. LeTourneau decided to open a plant in Toccoa, he did our community the greatest favor. Not only does the plant turn a weekly payroll of over $10,000 into our city, but the high moral standards of the LeTourneau personnel have added more than we can ever say to Toccoa's civic development.*
> The Toccoa Record

A North Carolina newspaper wrote,

> *We, the Christian laymen of the South, welcome this man of God into our midst ... What America needs so desperately is thousands of businessmen who will consecrate themselves and their businesses to God.*

Peoria theater marquee promoting Bob's speech: "Horsepower, Manpower, God Power"

He was alert for ways to use his God-given skills and resources. For more than 30 years, Bob boarded his plane on weekends and traveled to speak at churches and conferences, where he preached the gospel and told the story of how God called him to business.

One trip took him to a church in Tampa, Florida, pastored by the young Billy Graham. God used Bob's generosity to help launch and support the growth of Graham's worldwide ministry. The two were lifelong friends.

Bob with Billy Graham, 1953

He looked for ways to bring good out of tragedy. In 1940, a Toccoa company plane piloted by Bob's son, 19-year-old Don LeTourneau, crashed on the way to deliver parts to a customer in North Carolina. Bob worked out his grief over his son's death by building the best machines for the war effort, in hopes that he could help save other parents' sons on the front line.

He believed when God is your Business Partner, anything can be achieved. In 1953, at the invitation of the Liberian government, Bob sent earthmoving equipment to clear jungles, build roads and houses, and initiate economic development. He also established Bible-teaching programs that spawned churches across the country. He replicated the program in Peru at Tournavista.

As the first Christian businessman to personally finance overseas mission endeavors, Bob pioneered what is known today as Business as Mission. Rather than sending shiploads of aid to underdeveloped countries, he believed that helping people to become self-supporting was the best way to help them find God.

Members of the Tournavisa community in Peru outside their church building, 1965

We have a Wonderful Counselor on call 24/7.

Have you ever longed for a mentor who is always available to listen and advise you about decisions and challenges at work? Ideally, this individual would have firsthand experience and could offer wise counsel on workplace issues, such as how to deal with difficult people, how to handle financial setbacks and how to respond when you're asked to do something unethical.

The prophet Isaiah called Christ our Wonderful Counselor. He is always with us and promises to give us wisdom.

Prayer is the means of grace that connects us with God's wisdom, love and power—whether we're running a business, operating a forklift, managing a household or preaching a sermon.

> *If any of you lacks wisdom, he should ask God, who gives generously to all without finding fault, and it will be given to him. (James 1:5)*

7 Founding a University

*In 1940,
Bob was
interviewed
on "Ripley's
Believe It
or Not."*

Robert Ripley built a media empire by capitalizing on people's interest in the peculiar.

R. G. LeTourneau, as he was known professionally, was a perfect candidate for the show. Millions of listeners tuned their radios to hear Ripley interview the man who called God his Business Partner and gave away 90 percent of his income.

Six years later, Bob's story became even more extraordinary when the eighth-grade dropout founded what has become a world-renowned Christian university.

Believe it or not, here's how it happened.

After World War II, technology was changing, which prompted Bob to consider building another manufacturing facility and a steel mill. The venture required substantial open land and a nearby iron ore source.

The Longview, Texas area held promise, and at the invitation of Carl Estes, business leader and publisher of *The Longview News*, Bob and Evelyn traveled to East Texas to investigate.

Estes served as an aerial tour guide as they surveyed the region. When they flew over south Longview, Evelyn asked about a complex of white buildings stretched across sizable acreage.

Estes explained she had eagle-eyed the military barracks of Harmon General Hospital, 232 buildings on 156 acres, which the government decommissioned after the war.

Evelyn suggested to Bob that the property might work for their dream to start a school that offered technical training and traditional courses in a Christian environment to educate veterans returning from the war.

With their hearts ablaze and unified, Bob and Evelyn agreed to move to Longview and build a plant on two conditions. First, they needed to obtain the hospital property; and second, they

wanted the city of Longview to donate 10,000 acres of land to test LeTourneau machines, which was no small request.

Plus, they learned of another potential obstacle: Harmon General Hospital was classified "government surplus" and had to serve a purpose the United States government deemed acceptable.

Estes wasted no time. He sold the vision to East Texas moguls and flew to Washington to persuade government leaders. In less than three months, a deal was struck.

I had gone out hunting for a plant site adjacent to a steel mill, but the Lord wanted a school in which to train Christian engineers, and let me build my steel mill adjacent to it.

The government approved a technical school that would give veterans priority. The purchase price was only $1 dollar, but there were strings attached. No building could be removed or radically changed, and the government could reclaim the property, if necessary, within the first 10 years.

No stranger to risk, Bob trusted that his Business Partner was at work. On February 1, 1946, he and Evelyn held the keys to Harmon General Hospital, and the excited couple went to work.

Bob bulldozed the plant site while Evelyn and a cadre of helpers inventoried the 232 buildings. The acquisition did not include furniture or equipment, so she had to determine which items they should purchase to make the facility functional as a school.

On April 1, 1946, LeTourneau Technical Institute was dedicated to education for God's glory. The next day, classes began at the first school of higher education that combined formal study with practical application. The first work-study program of its kind allowed students to attend classes and work on alternating days at the LeTourneau plant, where they received hands-on experience and a paycheck.

We can only imagine the joy Bob and Evelyn experienced in 1961, when LeTourneau Technical Institute became LeTourneau College, a four-year coeducational school. In 1989, the college received accreditation as a nondenominational Christian university and embraced the name LeTourneau University.

Today, LeTourneau University is the premier Christian polytechnic university in the United States. Every aspect of a LeTourneau education is fueled by a vibrant, Spirit-driven passion to shape students who embody Christlike character and see their work as a holy calling with eternal impact.

The legacy of R. G. LeTourneau (1888-1969) and Evelyn LeTourneau (1900-1987) lives on through the university's unique emphasis on faith-work integration, hands-on education and Christian virtue—the three-fold core of the couple's original dream.

Living out one's faith requires both words and actions.

R. G. LeTourneau didn't just spout words about his faith, he lived them. He gave every day his best effort and trusted God for the outcome. He believed,

When the Lord has a job for you to do, He'll give you the strength and ability to do it.

LeTourneau dreamed big and took risks because he believed God can do immeasurably more than any entrepreneur can imagine.

Today, his legacy of faith, ingenuity and hard work blesses people around the world through the university that bears his name and its graduates, who take their faith to work in every workplace and every nation.

Now to him who is able to do immeasurably more than all we ask or imagine, according to his power that is at work within us ... (Ephesians 3:20)

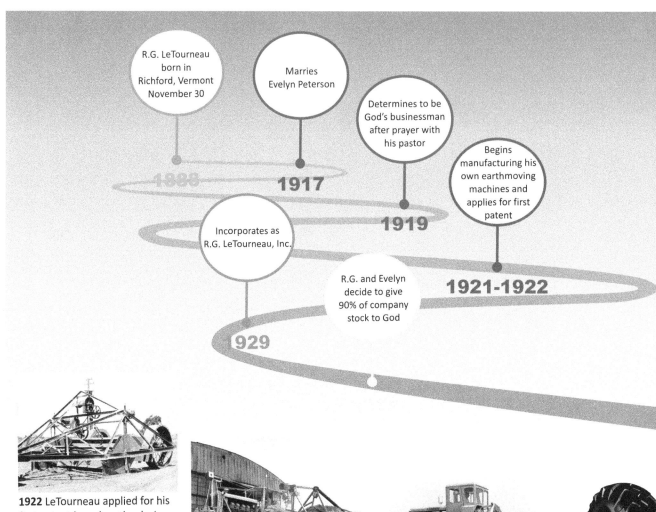

R.G. LeTourneau
born in
Richford, Vermont
November 30

Marries
Evelyn Peterson

Determines to be
God's businessman
after prayer with
his pastor

Begins
manufacturing his
own earthmoving
machines and
applies for first
patent

1888

1917

1919

Incorporates as
R.G. LeTourneau, Inc.

R.G. and Evelyn
decide to give
90% of company
stock to God

1921-1922

929

1922 LeTourneau applied for his first patent based on the design of the scraper known as the Gondola, built in Stockton, California.

1938 Model A Tournapull was the first rubber-tired prime mover.

1945 Model B Tournadozer was the first rubber-tired dozer.

1950 The Electric Wheel revolutionized earth-moving equipment.

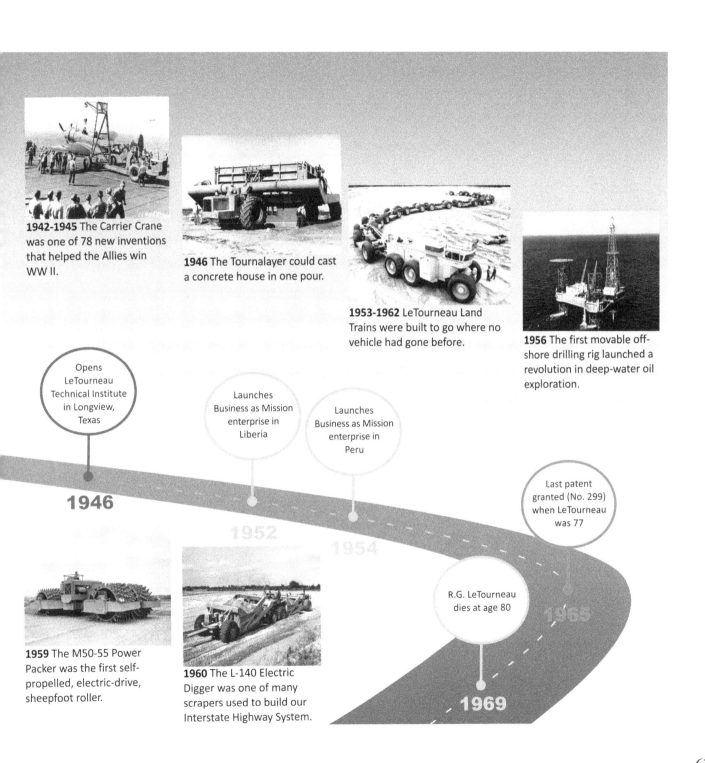

1942-1945 The Carrier Crane was one of 78 new inventions that helped the Allies win WW II.

1946 The Tournalayer could cast a concrete house in one pour.

1953-1962 LeTourneau Land Trains were built to go where no vehicle had gone before.

1956 The first movable off-shore drilling rig launched a revolution in deep-water oil exploration.

Opens LeTourneau Technical Institute in Longview, Texas

Launches Business as Mission enterprise in Liberia

Launches Business as Mission enterprise in Peru

Last patent granted (No. 299) when LeTourneau was 77

1946

1952

1954

R.G. LeTourneau dies at age 80

1965

1959 The M50-55 Power Packer was the first self-propelled, electric-drive, sheepfoot roller.

1960 The L-140 Electric Digger was one of many scrapers used to build our Interstate Highway System.

1969

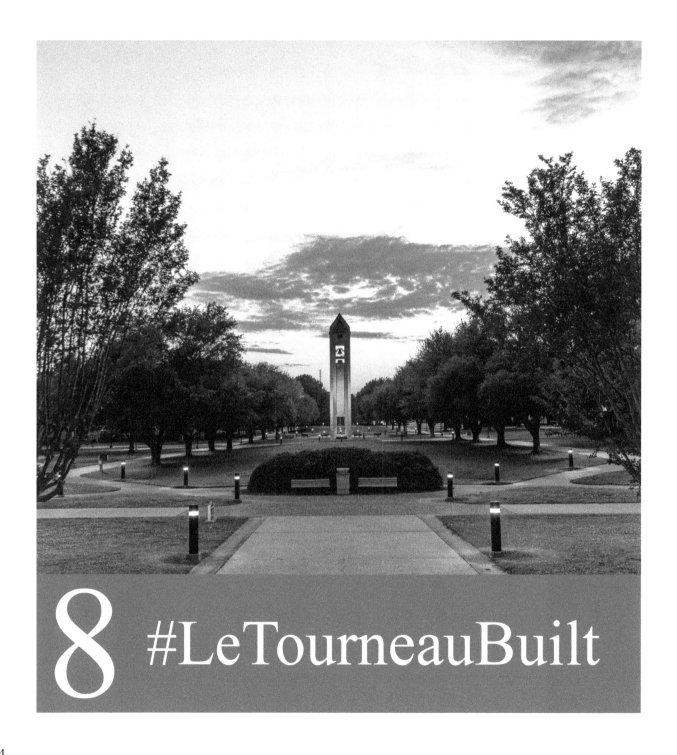

8 #LeTourneauBuilt

LETU is the *Christian Polytechnic University.*

Known for our distinctively Christian, hands-on approach to learning, LeTourneau University partners with students to discover God's vocational call and build their future.

Over 3000 students hale from states across the U.S., 30 foreign countries and represent 50 different denominations.

Consistently ranked in the top tier of "America's Best Colleges," LETU offers more than 140 undergraduate and graduate academic degree programs across a wide range of disciplines. Courses are available on-campus, online and in hybrid formats. Locations include the picturesque, 162-acre main campus in Longview, Texas, the East Texas Regional Airport and educational centers in Houston, Plano and McKinney, Texas.

Building Faith That Works

At LETU, spiritual formation is a holistic experience centered on shaping the mind, body and spirit of each student. Faith-enriching experiences—chapel services, class devotionals, faculty-guided small groups, community outreach programs, innovative mission projects—equip students to live their faith and share God's redemptive story with the world. LETU graduates build safer cities, establish strong companies, invent new products, develop new technology, heal the sick, pastor God's people, nurture young minds, restore broken relationships and work in countless other ways—all for God's glory.

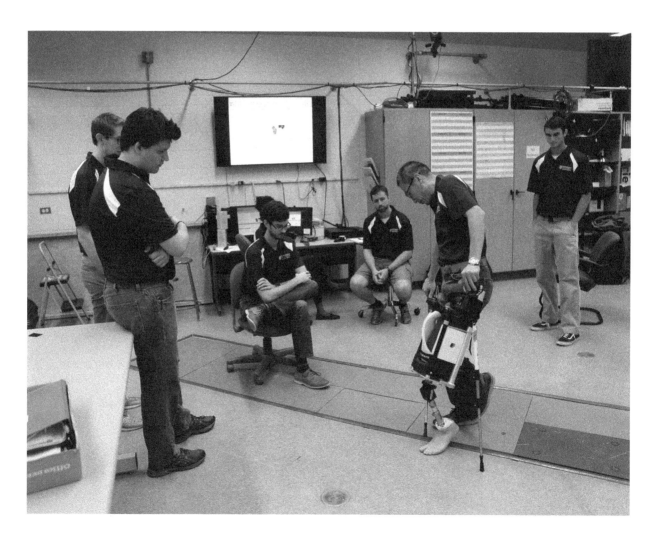

Called to Build

Prepared for their vocational calling by faculty and staff who deeply care for every student, LETU graduates go on to build careers, companies, communities, computer software, churches, equipment, technology and a host of products and services that promote human flourishing and care for God's creation. They also build relationships, fulfilling God's call to love our neighbor in courtrooms, classrooms, newsrooms, showrooms, operating rooms and break rooms by demonstrating competence, character, and sincere care for others at work.

Life-Building Community

At large universities, it's easy for individual students to become one more nameless face among hundreds—even thousands—in overflowing dorms and oversized lecture halls, where student-faculty interaction is rare.

Not so at LETU. Our faculty members are committed to building strong bonds with their students, not only as teachers and scholars, but also as friends and mentors who guide them to success in the workplace and all of life. They know students' names and often invite them into their homes for meals.

At LETU, students build friendships and a treasure trove of memories with faculty, staff and fellow students—and many become friends for life. LETU is community at its best.

Hands-On Learning

LETU's distinguished faculty bring years of industry experience to the classroom and continue our legacy of learning by doing. Students don't simply study theory and gain knowledge; they learn real-world applications by putting theory and knowledge to work.

In small classes, faculty provide personalized attention and create unique learning opportunities that prepare students to be leaders in their field. Applied research, interactive training, small-group discussions, collaborative design projects and collegiate competitions groom LETU graduates to enter the marketplace hardwired with hands-on experience. They're equipped to be problem-solvers in the local and global community— whatever their profession, wherever God leads.

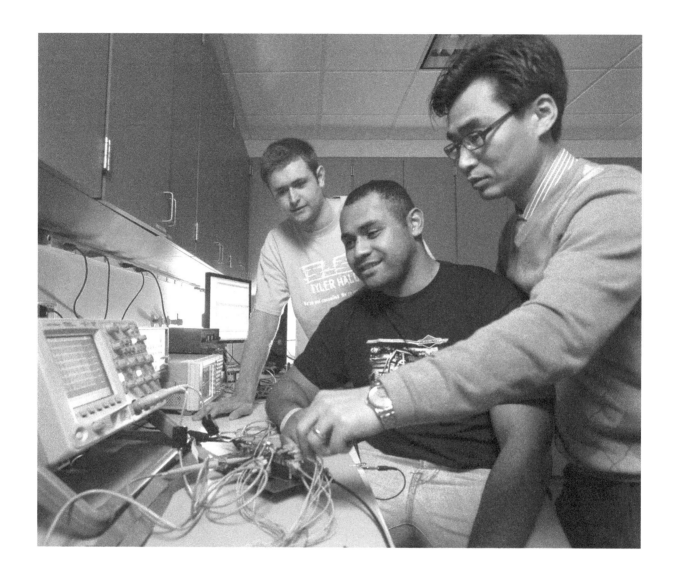

The School of Engineering & Engineering Technology

Known worldwide for our expert faculty, hands-on labs, student design projects and global research, LETU's rigorous portfolio of engineering disciplines includes civil, computer, electrical, biomedical, mechanical, environmental, materials joining, aeronautical-electrical and aeronautical-mechanical programs. Students are prepared to excel in their career, address challenging societal needs and build the world's future for God's glory.

College of Aviation & Aeronautical Science

LETU ranks among the top U.S. aviation training programs and offers the only comprehensive university-level aviation program in Texas. Our world-class Abbott Aviation Center at East Texas Regional Airport is the hub of operations, just 10 minutes from campus. Students study and learn from LETU's experienced faculty in state-of-the-art labs and fly airplanes maintained at the highest standards. Flight training and aviation management programs are also taught at LETU's facility at McKinney National Airport in North Texas.

The School of Nursing

The foundation of LETU's nursing program is a biblical view of healthcare that informs every course and shapes how students view nursing, today's healthcare issues and how they care for patients. In both our four-year residential program and our two-year RN-to-BSN online program, LETU nursing students develop the skills and proficiency needed to succeed in this high-demand profession and bring God glory in the work.

The School of Education

In the past decade, LETU has produced more teachers than any other private institution in Texas. Accolades and awards abound for graduates of LETU's School of Education, including many Texas State Teacher of the Year awards, Student Teacher of the Year Awards, a Clinical Teacher of the Year Award and numerous local teacher awards. LETU-trained teachers enjoy a 95 percent placement rate after graduation.

The School of Business

Building upon its history of esteemed STEM education and R. G. LeTourneau's legacy of innovative entrepreneurship, LETU's School of Business prepares students—both undergraduate and graduate—to uniquely shape the economic and ethical climate of the global marketplace. From year one, business students collaborate with future engineers, aviators, scientists and theologians to develop entrepreneurial solutions to global problems, capitalize on opportunities to build a better world and extend God's kingdom influence.

The School of Arts & Sciences

In a world where intellectual theories come and go, our Arts & Sciences faculty are the keepers of the flame of intellectual inquiry and eternal fundamental truth. They instill essential academic abilities into every course of study.

From the natural sciences and political science to communications and criminal justice, LETU programs cultivate students who use their gifts and acumen to engage and serve the world with professional excellence.

The School of Psychology & Counseling

Led by award-winning faculty with years of professional experience, LETU psychology and counseling programs are built on a Christian understanding of human nature, a holistic approach to wellness and a commitment to excellence in research and clinical training.

Equipped with expertise and practical experience, LETU graduates help people face life's challenges and live more functional and fulfilling lives. They bring a Christian perspective to the high-need, high-impact field of human behavior.

The School of Theology & Vocation

Our superior faculty guide all students to grasp their common missional calling to take the unchanging gospel to our changing world and help them discover their unique calling through thoughtful engagement between Scripture, academics and spiritual formation. Students called to vocational ministry are trained in the legacy of Christian leadership— not only to know the Bible, but to live it and train others, wherever God leads.

College years shape our life and our future.

Many parents and high-schoolers feel conflicted when choosing a college. They worry about campuses where hazing and promiscuity are the norm and professors scorn students of faith. But they also worry that Christian colleges isolate students from the "real world."

But one real-world truth applies at every college: Professors, curriculum and classmates have a powerful shaping force on a student's character, beliefs and worldview, which influence every aspect of life, both in and after college.

LETU is a learning laboratory for life where isolation is not an option.

Go therefore and make disciples of all nations, baptizing them in the name of the Father and of the Son and of the Holy Spirit, teaching them to observe all that I have commanded you.

Students, professors and like-minded classmates cheer each other on to build an exciting, fulfilling future as faithful Christ-followers who are poised for professional excellence and prepared to take the gospel to every workplace and every nation. As should we all.

9 The Center for Faith & Work

We equip Christians for their Monday morning mission field.

LeTourneau University created the Center for Faith & Work to preserve and promote its distinctive faith-work legacy in every aspect of college life and to fan the flame of today's global faith-work movement.

The Center works hand-in-hand with LETU leaders, trustees, faculty and staff to:

- ▸ Graduate Christian leaders who bring positive cultural change to their workplace and take the gospel to every workplace in every nation

- ▸ Provide continuing education and ongoing encouragement to more than 25,000 alumni, and help them connect with networks of other Christians who are living out their faith within their spheres of influence

- ▸ Inspire and equip the global Christian community to pursue their work as a holy calling

CENTER FOR
FAITH & WORK
at LeTourneau University

The history of western thought and civilization is dotted with men and women who challenged the erroneous assumption that some types of work are holier than others in God's eyes.

Martin Luther, John Calvin, John Wesley, Jonathan Edwards, Abraham Kuyper, Dorothy Sayers and R. G. LeTourneau, for example, urged Christians to recognize the value and sacredness of any and all work that promotes human flourishing.

The Center champions this truth and equips Christians in our common missional purpose in numerous ways.

ONLINE The Center's award-winning website offers over 1000 articles, interviews and resources about faith and work at CenterForFaithAndWork.com.

CURRICULUM We publish and co-publish books and create curriculum to help Christians understand their holy calling, honor God in their work, build businesses that glorify God and understand their legal rights.

I believe one of the next great moves of God is going to be through the believers in the workplace.
—*Dr. Billy Graham*

ON CAMPUS We bring exemplary professional leaders to campus to speak in chapel and interact with students.

PRESENTATIONS We customize compelling content about faith and work for keynote addresses, live workshops, sermons, podcasts and webinars.

LEADERSHIP We host, collaborate and provide leadership for local and global faith-work events.

CHURCHES We consult with churches to launch workplace ministries and equip congregants as ambassadors for Christ in the workplace.

VIDEO PROFILES We produce video interviews with business and professional leaders about how they live out their faith at work and build companies that bring God glory.

RESEARCH We commission and release landmark research on faith in today's workplace.

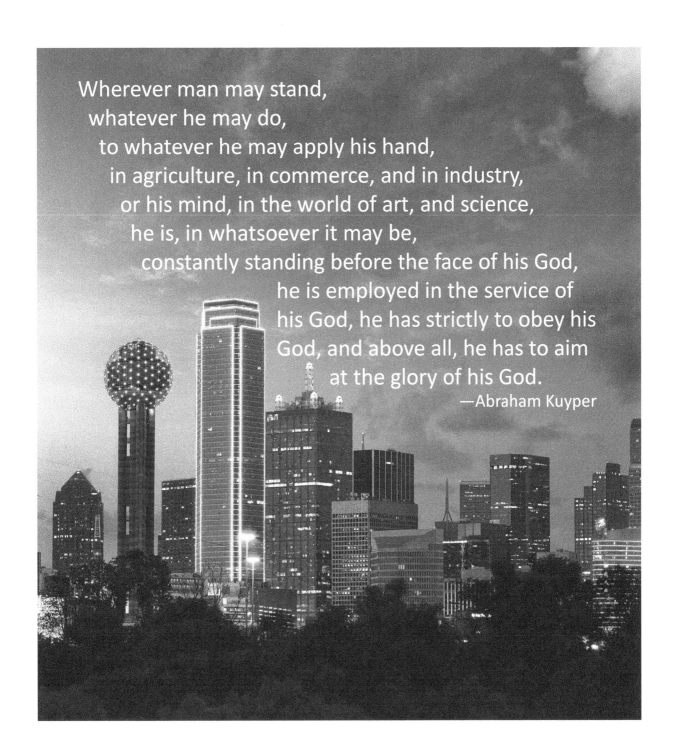

Wherever man may stand,
whatever he may do,
to whatever he may apply his hand,
in agriculture, in commerce, and in industry,
or his mind, in the world of art, and science,
he is, in whatsoever it may be,
constantly standing before the face of his God,
he is employed in the service of
his God, he has strictly to obey his
God, and above all, he has to aim
at the glory of his God.

—Abraham Kuyper

Acknowledgments

We sincerely thank the following people for their vital contributions to this book:

Dale Hardy, the unofficial R. G. LeTourneau historian and authority on all things R. G., checked historical facts and provided exclusive input.

Shelby Ware, LeTourneau University Librarian and Director of Margaret Estes Library and LeTourneau Historical Archives, helped us locate and identify important artifacts, photos and references.

Janet Ragland, Director of Public Relations at LeTourneau University, flagged errors, tidied content and offered invaluable encouragement.

Ivey Harrington Beckman, journalist and editor, brought helpful suggestions and expert corrections to the book in its early stages.

Dr. Dale Lunsford, LeTourneau University president, championed the formation of the Center for Faith & Work to carry on R. G. LeTourneau's legacy of integrating faith and work.

Credits

Select Bibliography

This list serves as a sampling, not a complete record, of the works and sources consulted to create this factual story that highlights defining experiences in R. G. LeTourneau's life.

Books

Carpenter, David. *A Passion for Partnering with God: Study Guide Based on Mover of Men and Mountains, The Autobiography of R. G. LeTourneau.* Wisdom Cries Out Publications, 2011.

Durham, Kenneth R. *LeTourneau University's First Fifty Years.* The Donning Company Publishers, 1995.

Gowenlock, Philip G. *The LeTourneau Legend.* Paddington Publications Pty. Ltd, 1996.

Hammond, Sarah Ruth. *God's Businessmen: Entrepreneurial Evangelicals in Depression and War.* University of Chicago Press, 2017.

LeTourneau, R. G. *Mover of Men and Mountains.* Moody Press, 1972.

LeTourneau, R. G. *R. G. Talks About: The Industrial Genius, Practical Philosophy, and Christian Commitment of Robert G. LeTourneau (1888-1969).* Edited by Louise LeTourneau Dick. LeTourneau Press, 1985.

Lorimer, Albert W. *God Runs My Business.* Fleming H. Revell Company, 1941.

Margolin, Efraim. *Building Dreams: Beer Sheva in 1949-1951.* N.p., 2012.

Orlemann, Eric C. *LeTourneau Earthmovers.* MBI Publishing Company, 2001.

Orlemann, Eric C. *LeTourneau Heavy Equipment.* Enthusiastic Books, 2014.

Rohrer, Norman B. *The Remarkable Story of Mom LeTourneau.* Tyndale House Publishers, 1985.

Stjernstrom, Nels E. *The Joy of Accomplishment: It's Always Too Soon to Quit.* LeTourneau University, 1989.

Articles and Journals

Jarman, Rufus. "LeTourneau: America's Most Spectacular Maker of Earth-Moving Machines Is 'In Partnership with God.'" *Life*, 16 Oct. 1944, 49-59.

Lee, Paul. "He's Changing the Face of the Earth." *Popular Mechanics*, May, 1955, 81-84, 238, 240, 242, 244.

May, Ashley. "Building Builders: A Christian Polytechnic University Takes After Its Inventive Founder." *Philanthropy*, Summer 2017. http://www.philanthropyroundtable.org

_____. "Enterprise: The Monster-Maker." *Newsweek*, 16 Nov. 1959, 89-92.

Stuart, David R. "Earthmoving Capital of the World: San Joaquin County's Agricultural Needs Led to Decades of Innovation." *The San Joaquin Historian*, Summer 2017. http://www.sanjoaquinhistory.org

Wharton, Don. "Heaven and Earth Man." *The Reader's Digest*, March, 1944, 99, 100-101, 107.

About the Author

Kathy Peel is a journalist, award-winning author of 22 books and popular speaker at churches, conferences, colleges and companies around the world.

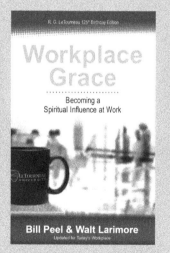

LETU.edu

CenterForFaithAndWork.com

CPSIA information can be obtained
at www.ICGtesting.com
Printed in the USA
LVHW070835070720
659750LV00017B/879